MÉLISANDE FITZSIMONS

SKYLARK

STOAT BOOKS

SKYLARK

ISBN: 978-1-918724-04-2

POCKET SERIES

04

First published 2026

Edited by Leona Franke

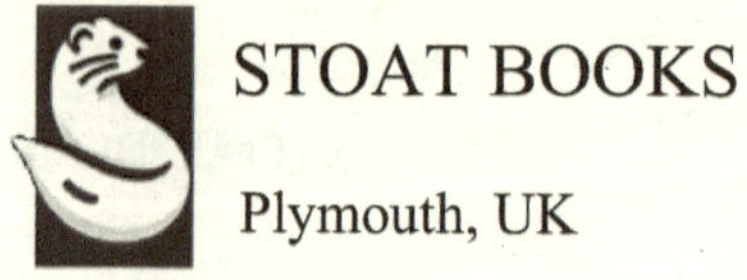

MÉLISANDE FITZSIMONS

Skylark is a daring, polyphonic meditation on language, memory, and the strange music of modern history. Mélisande Fitzsimons moves between myth and reportage, elegy and experiment, drawing new correspondences between the body, the state, and the stories we inherit.

This is a collection of restless intelligence and deep compassion — where history speaks through hippos and coronations, through bombed cities and buried kin. Fitzsimons writes with wit, fury, and lyric precision, weaving voices that refuse containment and refuse to forget. There are no clear borders here — only fracture, chorus, and the wild persistence of speech itself.

OTHER BOOKS:

Sirène, 2017

A Language of Spies, 2019

Tomorrows, 2021

The Only Country in the World, 2023

POEMS

Phoenix

Flirtation separates steam from sand turns crude water into conversations. Gearheads play bomber boys with little lies like *yeah Egyptian blue's a make, fast sports crate like Alfa naffy Romeo all self, selfself, super ego-man named after a car, pull factor's still a Lambo, way too expensive, knowwotmsayin?*

They think they are right because they are boys but boys are just random variables a bit unpredictable after a few drinks in a country full of cars growing to ridiculous lengths

At Penderyn in split-arse turns and spins the fireproof cowboys line up to drive their heaps into the water taking selfies while the alloys spray crowns all over the crowd #hellovaflush

Hooshing in the smoke trails they fight and dream they drive for danger grab a piece of nice making out on the synthetic back where the lines send back reflections and shadows on the window

Try it with a torch. Try a dirty reflector. Time the melting. What load will it carry here unnamed before the car is slammed into collapse? Does width make a difference to strength? Expansion can cause problems. Note where the weakness in the limbs is. Shake to a regular beat. How difficult is it to do it well?

One thing is sure they get hot. Be careful of toes and joints. Very large forces are at work; the joints are often the weakest parts but arched limbs will bend and spring back. The tongue is a lover's best friend it gets in the way of breath and sound makes sense of the supercharged song hearing the jammed frequencies in a variety of higher notes to create new tones

There's something so valuable under the surface where every conversation is left underground unseen but alive. A bright white corona is discharged around the spot blood flushes through the cracks, combines danger and wonder so well packing a 1-2 punch

the fur moves

Spilling through saturation of patterns reaches unearthed strong riches. The spur always comes up from hiding. As you tilt the gauge remove the skin parchment layers of nerves push the moving fluid as a sign to say yes I do

Leaving behind dreams of wildfire and flight magicians the girls make do with old oil burners. Live hot water just pours from their mouths like marvels. One tongue spits teases the others one language eats another. Don't kneel yet. The boys too cool to say complete words will have to wait: the performance won't match their looks anyway

In the starmy night ebullition carries the line of their lips. There are two or more bluebirds in that car a bubble dancing on a sandy track in the old workings hidden in a corner behind Cleft Woods and deeper marches beyond tailing ponds and waste sludge. They use mounds for pillows small debris of stone elfstones elf-shot light a steady fire for home pathfinders far from a land of signs

They remain still in halting yes and clouds of fume. The interrupted forces of their bodies which carry the power of chaos release enough space for the outline of a river tracing the fabulous letters of their names. Who will they be after kissing when they tear down to the cold-water tap of home?

They convoy home thinking *shit, what time is—oh fuck, I'm gonna get hell again*

One of Us

1. Plural

I live in a country proud to spend millions pumping up a Trident of pomp, quiche and stirring music. The Liverpool fans who booed the national anthem are lucky: in the days when subjects wore the king in their wallets royalty didn't always take kindly to a distaste for the monarchy.

It was a triumph a milestone between Dublin and London: The Irish Delegation set precedent by showing respect to Britain. Alas VIP Matt didn't get the memo. He kept his phone on and boyfriend Leo was filmed picking his nose just as the queen consort touched the Sceptre and Rod. Red faces all around. What a symbolic gesture for Ireland!

2. Singular

Surrounded by a wet Union and inflatable crowns the Upholder of the Protestant Faith in Divine Right mutters as he goes past in his gold carriage (fitted with electric windows)

Yes I am
we can never be
on time
there is always
something
this is so boring

Oh the very heavy lifting of that crown! Ah but he doesn't have to smell us he doesn't have to feel our sweat and it's all on us.

3. Protest

Police police here we come. Acting on intelligence they arrested fifty-two people for possession of strings and luggage straps. The straps will be used for a locking-in protest create havoc and panic in a vile plot to spook kings and horses. That's the drama of a terrorist swoop.

Protest arrest a farcical case unrest. How do you ensure the situation doesn't escalate? We were just there to avoid the coronation miles away after tracking the Croydon Cat Killer. It was a day of intense learning for everyone. They were all talking at once: *You're under arrest*. Why? *Do not sip your coffee it could be poisoned or something.* I asked for a solicitor and was served a vegan all-day breakfast instead which was literally ALL beans. I want my phone and watch back, says Matt.

The police have declined to comment.

Dead or Alive

I

Pablo's hippos are dead on the road
waste excretors an invasive species
attackers on the rise viral capybara
killers victims

Ask Pepe what he thinks. The short
answer? Public opinion

Are they very large and aggressive
exterminators interested persons
animals with personhood status in the
US animal rights mascots a
challenge to gun rights groups?

Also known as Pablo's pets frivolous
trophies ecological time bombs they
were the lucky residents of Hacienda
Napoles while it lasted (now a theme
park)

A target for culling or castration
spreading cocaine-like catastrophe as
they mate still inspiring pity (the
weather also helps) they tipped the
crane

II

We are talking about animals that can weigh 5 tonnes like the dinosaurs in Jurassic Park. They are not a bit cute. They kill communities. A hippo skin is bulletproof. It can be removed with a zipper located underneath the torso

If you plan on shooting a hippo your best bet is to induce it first. 94% of people have seen hippos in the wild. Their skulls make great decorations in gardens. A coffee table made from a skull with a glass top looks nice

The leather skin of a hi**o makes great shoes purses cartridge belts shooting bags satchels. But I have never seen the feet used. Just finding it somewhere on the internet. It's the actual hide not a repro. Don't hesitate to ask

Use your imagination, it's fun!

III

I have taken many out due to using them for great lion bait. Do not mount them as the repros are far better. I had the skins tanned in two colours (primitive and powder) and gave a set of teeth to my dentist. Murray made me some gun cases/ knife sheaths/ and custom boots

Somebody asked me why I had shot so many h*p*os. Because I am a lousy lion hunter, is why! Any use for the feet? I have seen el**ha*ts turned into stools. Has anyone had their hides made into more “practical” items? Thought it might be cool to make gear from some, but wondering about the cost

Could we have the hides dip-packed and then shipped to the States for processing? On a side note: I posted this question before but I didn’t get much of a response. Interesting... I think it’s a good idea to have a plan for your skins, unless they are back skins and you have a plan for their use

I got mine loaded on a repatriation flight last week as outbound cargo. Anything you want: backpacks duffle bags inlays bench seats for a pickup things for the wife Your imagination is the limit. Best of luck

Wounds: a Meticulous Observation of my Left Hand in Sixty Minutes or Less

I sliced my middle finger with a tin of duck during an argument with my flatmate about their supremacist dad then observed the delay between the *Aaaïïïïïe* sucking great ribbons of my salty blood and the pain. At the hospital they sewed the wound with a Soviet needle and thread:

no anaesthetic

the nurse was really fit and cheerful, chattering about astrology and Italy while stitching the flaps of my skin. We shared the same star sign: Jupiter in Mars was behind all this we agreed. He was obviously distracting me from the pain. He tried to keep me very still, but I craved his touch a charge as erotic as a good subtitle. If you look closely, a white arrow tiny scissors or is it a fork are visible below the first knuckle

this hand has lines of love and indecisiveness which change texture when you arch the skin back. Ooooh, we don't want to mess with you, said Mo stroking my palm before promising a tea-leaves reading that never happened

I'd slashed my little finger with the pocketknife

straight blade/pale horn-tip handle/bee-incrusted spring/the shape and texture of memory

that my grandmother who lived on vodka and sliced lemons before breathing her last on a cruise to Egypt without so much as one last word, just the slightest of sighs, had given me on my 10th birthday. The scar has morphed into a dit and a dah an embossed M then an en a brève scar on either side of the joint face

I kept that knife safe for years went with it on twelve moves through France and

England then my son loses it on a walk
in Wales

you lost the only thing she gave me how
can I ever forgive you

Haiku

no man-made slate to
be thrown at the monks under
no circumstances

little rust comets
slowly explode at my feet
a very cold day

do you want to be
my mother? My heart leaps yes!
no, she said model

Italics *pleins et*
déliés such spirit in
one simple font

packed the birdfeeder
with worms bodyguard seagulls
peck magpies away

was to, would become
when became is just so much
better in my view

against the light I
shake the tree expecting a
tiny miracle

my siblings, will I
be the first to go? I dare
not say it aloud

in a garden for
quiet poetry I am
the loudest of course

in her wardrobe I
choose her last winter coat, still
silent for so long

J'espère she says sadly
he has no French. Rain falls
in and out of water

Eden, I am lost.
In paintings, it always is
an apple. Wrong. Fruit
with seeds they could eat: I am
very keen on quince's bite

Alone in her Prison Cell Aliénor d'Aquitaine Reflects on the Randomness of Language and History

England England land of sputum and spit I love it. I have always loved your spirit even when your buttery tongue licked me into near losing the deep fur, felt sounds of my own. Against the plastic colourful surging of Worcester Gloucester always talking about the weather I still carry la fleur folie ardeur of my years in o© ad ho© o for yes. O: c'est cela © silent a sacred yes it is-o-il est.

It is true to say that no English people are ever foreign. Your tongue crept up on me like silk while mine was elsewhere in some so-near abroad that I remember with large gaps an incomplete text rising into the air. It's the same litany: Leicester lestée delestée sorry so sorry ever so sorry but where is your blood? Then young Henri "coeur de marbre" Plantagenêt dumb as a bag of hammers has me locked up forever. History is a lot sweatier and less well dressed than in books.

Aliénor alien nation, aliénation. Pigeon-holed in prison I grow roots like wood holds knots. The book that rests on my hands holds messages without visible words a tree sending signals to other trees. Motionless arrested against the light I chart down the discomfort of pinched shoulders and a stiff back. At dusk when the only company I face is short shadows it's a bless to be sitting on a lion for strength. Less in more depth. I will probably outlive him.

Aliénor au Coeur d'Alène with a long history of protesting even finds herself entangled in new words like a bird caught on a limed branch: it's easy for a foreigner to lose her voice. Sounds I make with the tongue mid-mouth will suddenly come up from hiding like explosives. But also the fun of mimicry the animal electricity so feared by wolves of faking language for my jailers: there is a lot of dance in the movement of that mouth. Somehow I know I am heading towards a cliff top sink until it becomes more fluid a flamer a souffle thistle.

This is called developing a language scent. There's something secure in that perseverance like the return of the river in the middle of the poem when the flow of water turns one moment into something far more impulsive. Winter veers towards the water a liquid metal carrying the heft of light. The memories are just air that live within the intensity of print sublimed when warmed. When spring comes we look back and carve out random lines in the sand. Dead voices must be allowed to keep their silence too.

On a Short Visit to Ireland We Bury Skylark my Brother-in-Law

No entry/car park exit this way. No parking in front of gates. No access except for Girl Guides. No unauthorised parking. Only authorised access to cars with permits. Parking in front of the gates is prohibited. No parking at any time. Garage in constant use. Please no. Please no thank you. Shoplifters will be prosecuted. Fasten your seat belt while seated. Life vest under your seat. Safety onboard. Keep left. Car hire deliveries return.

Remove your belt. Remove your shoes. Go through the glass machine, one at a time. Lift your shoe. And the other one. Take off your shoe and each other. Are you wearing your seat belt? Remove your scarf. Remove your toiletries from the bag. What's your name, Sir? Open your passport at the right page. Show your boarding card. Don't forget your receipt. Cabin luggage. Taking pictures of the crew is strictly prohibited. You can't pay by cash. No engines left running. Evacuating positions.

One way only, restricted parking. The toilets are at the back of the plane, two exits at the front two exits at the back. Change machine. You must be 21 to enter the arcades. Ticket machine. Exchange tickets for a prize. Dodgems. Wedding area upstairs. £3.00 for soda water. Three British pounds! I'm sorry cash only. We've run out of tea. Ladies at the back. Reserved for families and friends. Video link to the Lady of Assumption (live). The blind is remote-controlled. The boys were so well-behaved during Mass.

Stevie he she they at the nursing home calls me love. I don't mind, he-she-they say. I am a stepbrother a sister mixed race. Mixed heritage, you mean? Yes. Calls me wee pet. They are all fighting for the dog. It barks when you pat the head. We wrote her name on the collar just in case. The light changes and the Mournes keep growing. The clouds over the promenade become a conversation piece. That or a frozen smile. Celebrity Catchphrase on ITV1. I can't hear you. The owner had it especially commissioned. It's painted from the sea.

When we don't get paid we peel off the gold from the ceiling. The incessant ring of the alarm. We don't register to get in we know the code. Anne stares with dark eyes. Blind but you wouldn't know at first.

A very early start. No wipes. Ulster is British. No UK internal border. I will say a prayer for you and for your family. Prepare to meet thy God. East Belfast. Ballynahinch. Carryduff. Seaforde. Clough. British Springtime. Fast food joints everywhere all over the world. Where is the brake on this thing? We couldn't shut the blind. It's remote operated. We didn't know. Bridges everywhere and little sign of peace. Small signs of peace. The daffodils are out. The boys were so well-behaved during Mass.

Rocket came back home last month with one leg hanging off. The builders wrapped him in a towel and placed him in a cat carrier. Cost me £300 at the vet to have its leg removed. Can't hop on the counter anymore. We were going to call him Biden. Father Jim is a prickly man. You can't say that when you never go to Mass. We wouldn't like to do his job. We both noticed he had communion now we know which foot he kicks with.

My son could eat a whole chicken in one sitting. Ireland is so backwards. At least in Dubai we had access to everything in one place. I'm not drinking. It's Lent Guinness 0%. I am going slightly crazy. Far too many cars in town people in the forest park. Let the river have her say. The Girl Guides hollering in the distance. Why not try something different? Sprite is like 7UP. Thank you for your patience. The view over the Mournes. Gorgeous boys show me your football cards. What team do you support? It's been years. You look amazing. I love your hair. You are the only French woman I know. Your wife was immediately at ease with me. Quite a remarkable lady. Residential area please switch off engines and no horns. Beware traffic queueing ahead. Staff car park authorised personnel only.

Haven't forgotten about the recording. I love your lipstick. Gavin and Michael could be twins. At least it's not raining.

Four seasons in one. Which school do they go to? England. What's the name of the school? What's the name of their school? We are now flying over Anglesey. A very early start. It's been a pleasure to fly with you. So well behaved during the service. We are waiting for air control to take off. We have enough fuel in an unlikely event. Ten minutes to landing. The blinds must be opened. Stow away in front of you. Before landing, complete check of the cabin.

And you Skylark right in the vastness of the Assumption all but contained in that little box of ashes.

Fuck eternal life. That startled a few of them. We want life now sacred Heart of Jesus. Holy candles in the pound shop. The boys were so well behaved at the ceremony. Chains on the High Street same all over the world. Herrons aka the original KFC. Litter. The charity shops are the same everywhere. They keep smiling. Very. All that grass in Saint Patrick's churchyard and cherry trees in blossom. Back to England green land.

Drab houses. We are running out of fuel. Have it.

Three seagulls perched on a car rooftop heads and beaks tilted to drink dew. A brutal landing. No electronic devices allowed until inside the airport area. Ten minutes ahead of schedule. Strong smell of gasoline. Propeller plane. A bientôt the only French I know. Hasta la vista. Arrivals. Police control. Sanitise. Automatic doors. Domestic flights only. Stay safe. Keep safe. Keep two metres apart. Wash your hands for twenty seconds. Will you two stop fighting for a minute? Now wash your hands for twenty seconds. No wipes. Your hair is beautiful. Charges apply. Leave this place as you found it.

I Asked You

what you had seen printed in the rock face in ochre and spit

you said: uranium

which can be sung and used for sorcery

but without the song it is just a white rock

carrying the trace of its
burning

metals will bend and swing back, and like us some will stay bend, or squat

like tanks:

some substances don't get easily consumed

Draconic Beasts

the basic desire is to believe that plants
and animals are

alike and have
memories

plants are strange organisms
depicted in modern legend as bladed
creatures

in the absence of nerves they
have arrows everywhere to
everything

as well as wounded
leaves that provide

beautiful images

when injured with forceps

they have been known to
set the surrounding area

ablaze

Lithium

in the Atacama beauty the desert
appears an overwhelm

in brown and scaly colours that
clings to salty

bones reaching like fingers
against the sky fizz
and bang

when they meet water
and air

cracking always starts at the
edges sometimes

formed like a found object
a curiosity

a burst of flames
visible from space

Lithium as a pale blue
liquid, discord-bright neon

manifests in
songs added to
drinking
water

and triggers the odd shape of a chemical

explosion: you get the idea

Everything is Shallow and Full of Remote Fortunes: Three Years On

Amiss: a missile landed; it left a seven-metre crater. Apart from the war going on not much has changed. It's 14 degrees Celsius in the lab so some reagents freeze and we need to adapt to power cuts. With the next shelling the power cuts are less predictable. Is this a reflection of Britain not knowing what it is anymore? It was so much easier when I was born. We knew what our role in the world was and had huge pride in what we had achieved. That, coupled with Wales' truly awful rugby record this year makes me wonder whether a very prolonged cruise in my boat might be more pleasurable.

We hope to keep having a warm winter until March because I don't know what we'll do if it was minus 20 degrees Celsius for a week or two. Men still can't leave Ukraine. I sit under the stairs with my son at home. I work with high pressure reactors jokingly called bombs. Jenny is still on the church Parish council though she will step down next year. Flower Club is still important to her. I have had a good year with orchids particularly with Cymbidiums as they require different conditions. One is grown in the greenhouse and the other in our conservatory. The Dendrochilliums produce beautiful chains of flower at least once a year and my Brassias never fail me.

Chirping: the frequency of a pulse changes as a function of time. Two images produced from one object seems like magic. How surreal a big city looks with close to zero streetlights on. It's worrying when the air raid siren starts during work. Jenny's memory is poor but we continue happy and it has not stopped us sailing. Neither has my arthritis which is a bit worse so we both continue with full and happy lives. My arthritis did cause me to move to an SUV from my saloon car. It was getting too difficult to get in and out particularly in car parks.

There are fewer blackouts on Saturdays which is nice like a window into a normal life. There are no spare parts nobody listened when we asked the

West for help with equipment. We need to use helium pipelines made of PVC tubes. When the temperature is low the tubes shrink and the helium just leaks. The boat gave us a problem this summer. It developed a series of electrical problems which completely disrupted our holiday. We corrected the electrical problems but this winter I hope to improve the electrical system quite a bit. I've also started taking up the floor and revarnishing the floor panels. The removal of the varnish has to be done in my garden so fine weather is needed.

I videoed a bolide fireball brighter than the full moon. It had a fusion crust bluish-purple iridescence and it was a fragment of meteorite which only exists naturally in minute traces. We look forward to Christmas and the new year. We do the same thing every year but still enjoy it; we hope you all have an enjoyable Christmas and New Year too.

Spells/Vote *(After the State of Louisiana Literacy Test 1964)*

spell backwards forwards write right from the left

to the right as you see it spelled here

print the word vote upside down but in the correct order

write right from the left to the right as you see it dispelled here

draw five circles that one common inter-locking part (sic)

above the letter X make a small cross

So *(Cree, Florida 2023)*

this what the jail house doing

go on to see my brother release date

and this what I see

after all these years this

the best they can do

sex: M

race: B

<u>ethnicity: N</u>

Eyes: BRO

In the Space

below

write the word   noisebackwards

divide it in half and place a dot

over what would be its third letter

should it have been written forward

divide it once more by drawing a broken

line from the middle of its eastern

side to the middle of its western side

Blitz

We went back to the house with my friend. We were the posh ones because we still had a bit of railing in front. The whole of the ceiling rose in the front room had come down. There was another blast. If you could imagine a big bowl of rice, lift up the rice and let it run inside the jar, that's incendiaries coming down, hundreds of them at a time. A couple of sailors picked us up and carried us to what was left of the front window to see the flames and said: 'you will never see a sight like this again.' The whole of Devonport was ablaze.

She just sat at her piano and played, my mum, and would not go into any shelter or protect herself. Once there was a blast and she ended up with Venetian blinds all around her. Oh, she did look funny! There was muck all over the piano, and she was still playing away. Dad wouldn't come in the shelter either, he'd stay roaming around the house while she played, ready with his tongs to throw out bombs when they came in.

A blind couple lived next door to us. They went down in the air raid shelter with us and when we got up next morning their house was gone. Later the blind woman said: ‘I can still smell it now, the stuff from all the fires and all the rubble, an awful stale smell, like burnt hair, vermin, mice, fleas. All that’. When a house is hit by a bomb, it releases a peculiar smell. It's like its life has gone. It’s a smell that I have never forgotten.

The Germans scored a direct hit on the oil tanks at Turnchapel. One bomb fell in our garden. We had a fishpond, and the next morning the windows were all blown in and the fish were dead, scattered all over the garden with all sorts of old cable reel, all odd bits and pieces. Going back into the house, I hated it. I was afraid there was a German there, waiting for me.

I could hear the planes up there, the bombs were coming down, this sailor threw himself over me to protect me, and then I lost my new hat. You could see the aircraft, the search lights on the aircraft and the ack-ack guns having a go at them, like the gun was right beside you. The whining whistle of the bombs

coming down, and then the shuddering, and us holding each other. Howl dogfights in the sky everyone pray, I was hanging on to my brothers and sisters like stones.
All the men at Pottery Quay were running in and out of our houses and passing buckets full of water down the passage, to go and put the fire out across the road. The tides used to be so high, the spring tide, the water come right in our front room and there was two big swans swimming in the front room who'd come in with the tide.

After Eileen Organ, Vera Evans, Michael Turpitt, Val MacLeod, Sheila Allen, Sheila Soroka, Peter Amey, Maggie Daniels, Susan Wills, Fred Brimacombe, Desmond Robinson, Colin Baser, Arthur Rugg, Barry Woon, Mr Ward, Mrs Hancock, Angela Watts, with thanks.

Acknowledgements

Thanks to the editors of the following journals, who first published these poems: *Culture Matters, International Times, Lay of the Land, Stride, Tears in the Fence* and *The Fortnightly Review.*

I am very grateful to Leona Franke and Thom Boulton for their editorial support and dedication.

www.ingramcontent.com/pod-product-compliance
Lightning Source LLC
LaVergne TN
LVHW051022080826
845145LV00009B/2759

* 9 7 8 1 9 1 8 7 2 4 0 4 2 *